I0485298

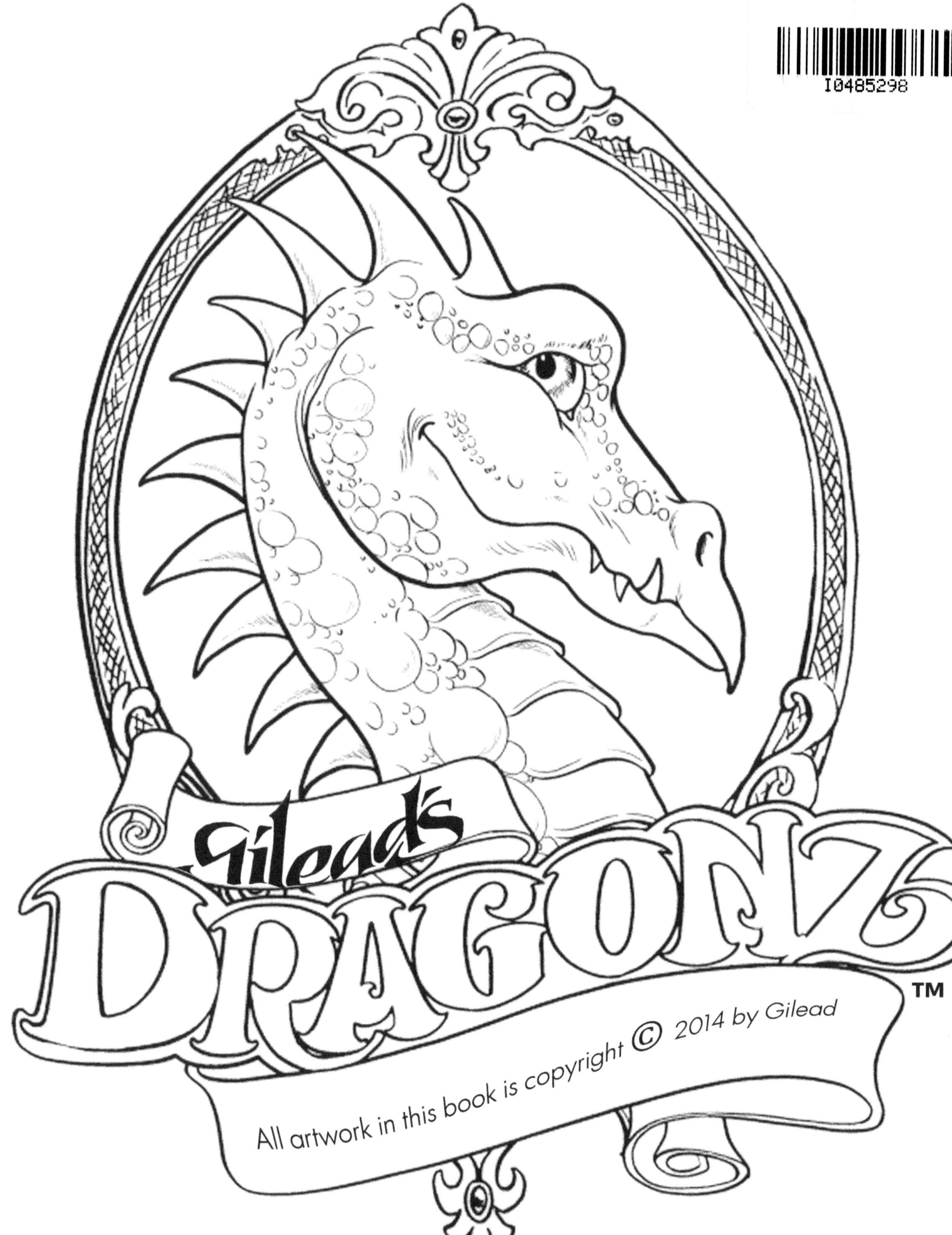
Gilead's
DRAGONZ™
All artwork in this book is copyright © 2014 by Gilead

Made in U.S.A.

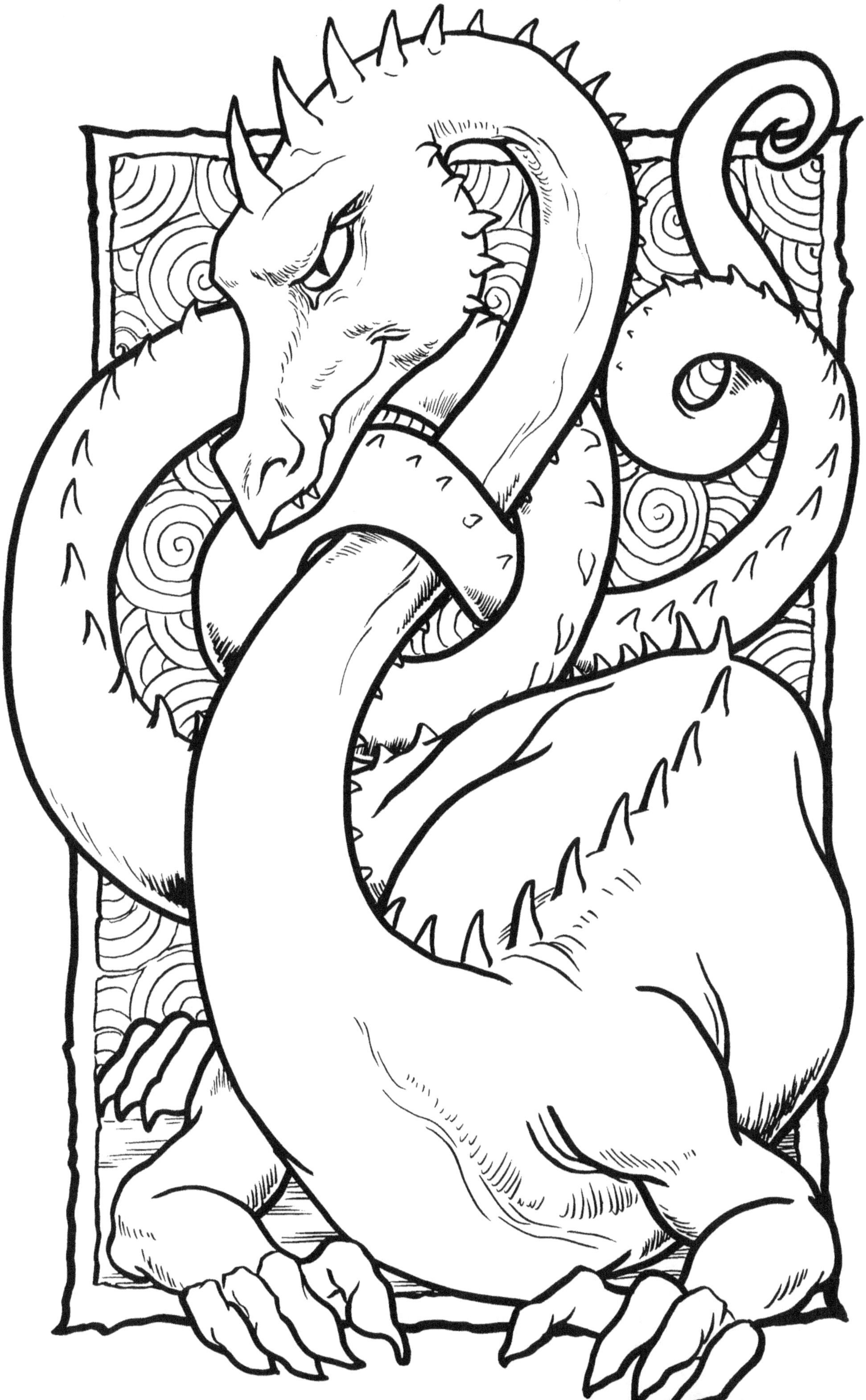

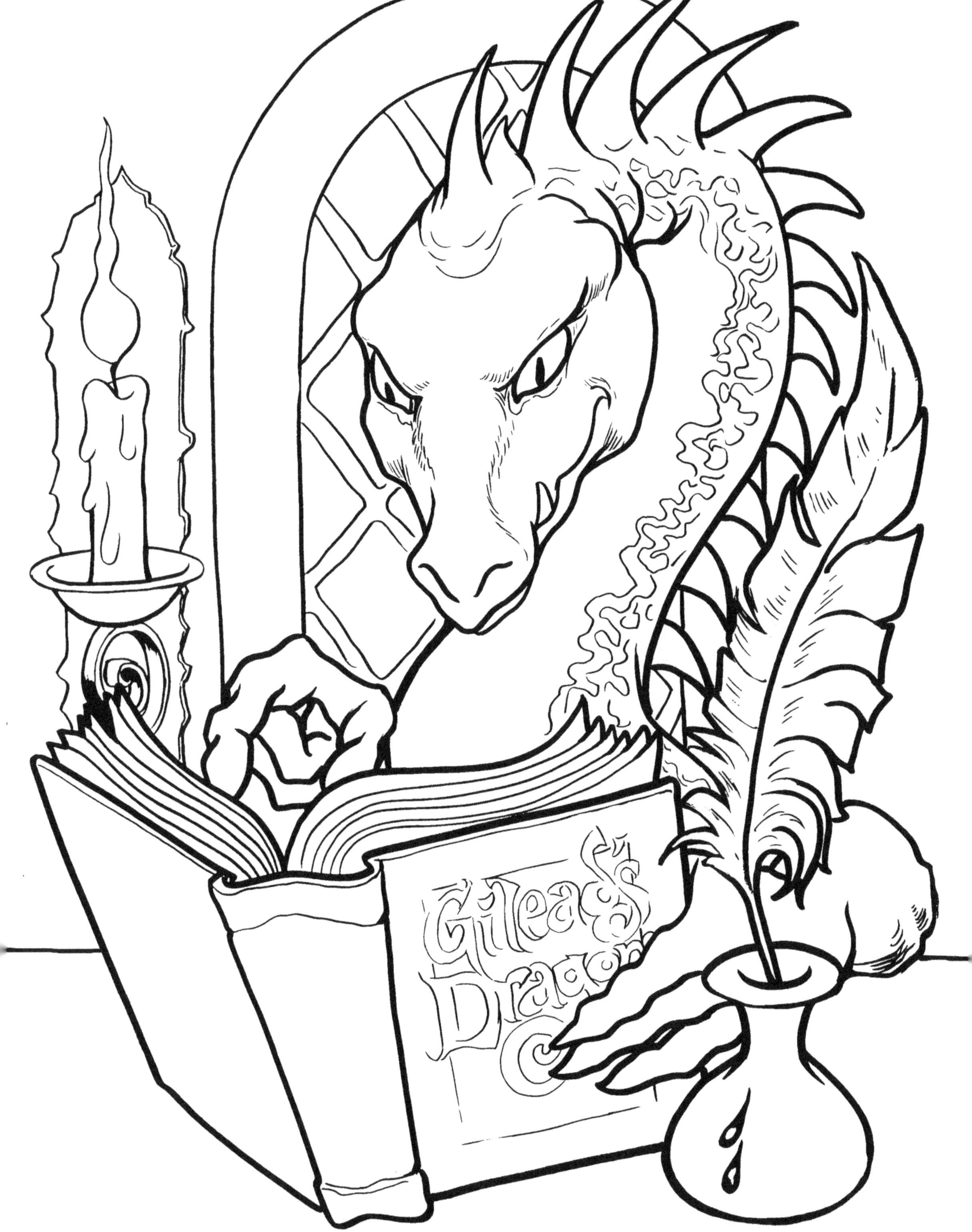
Gilead's
Dragons

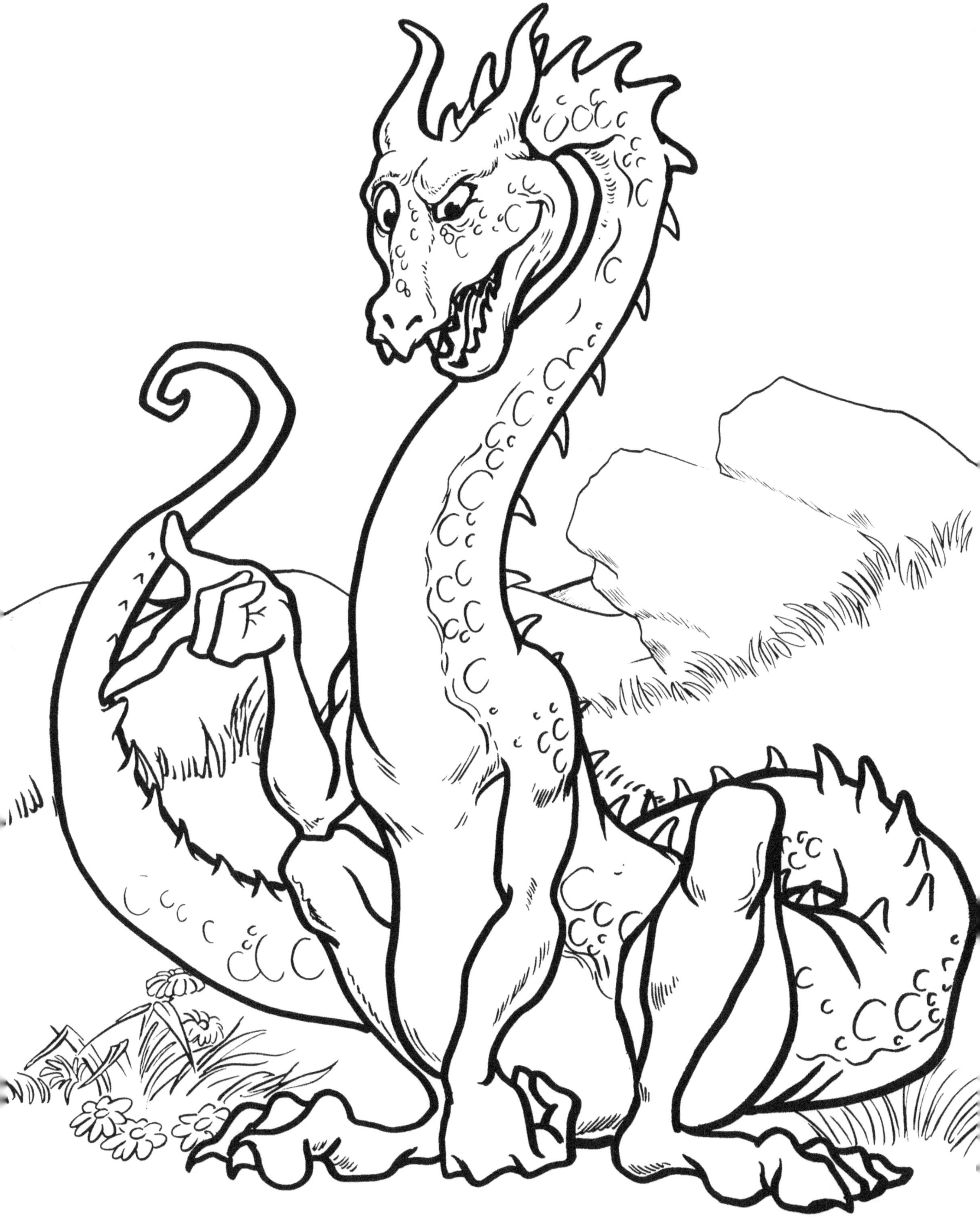

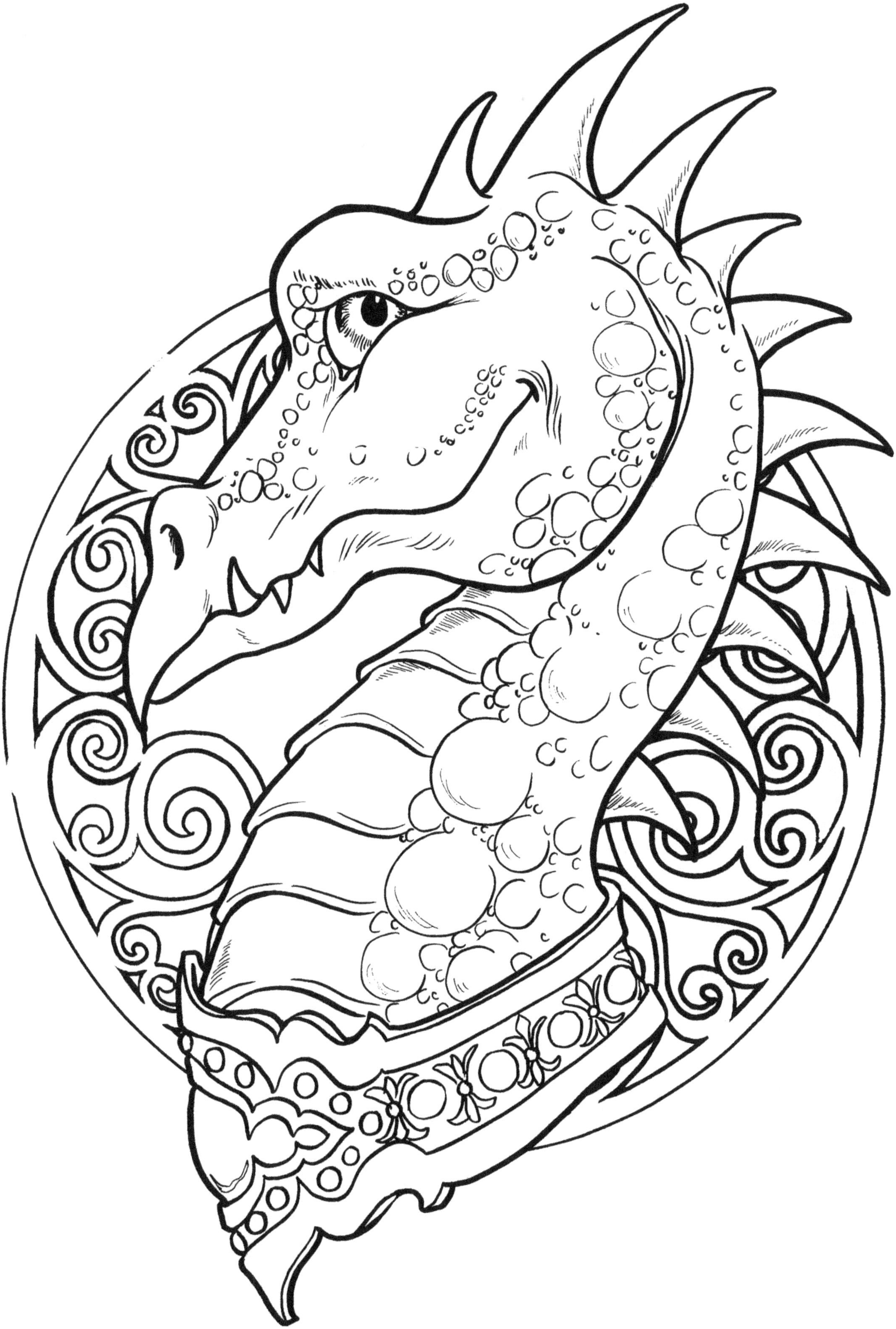

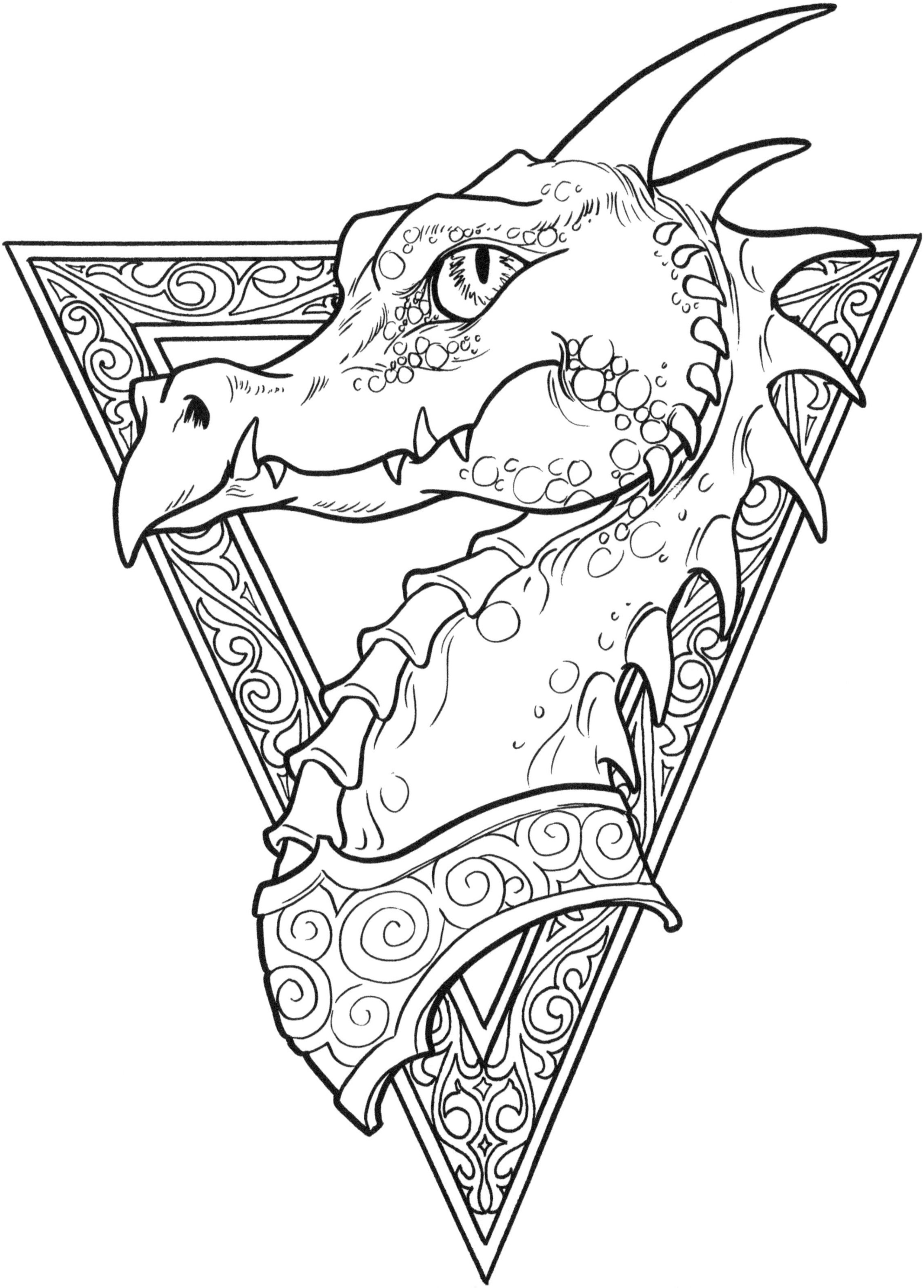

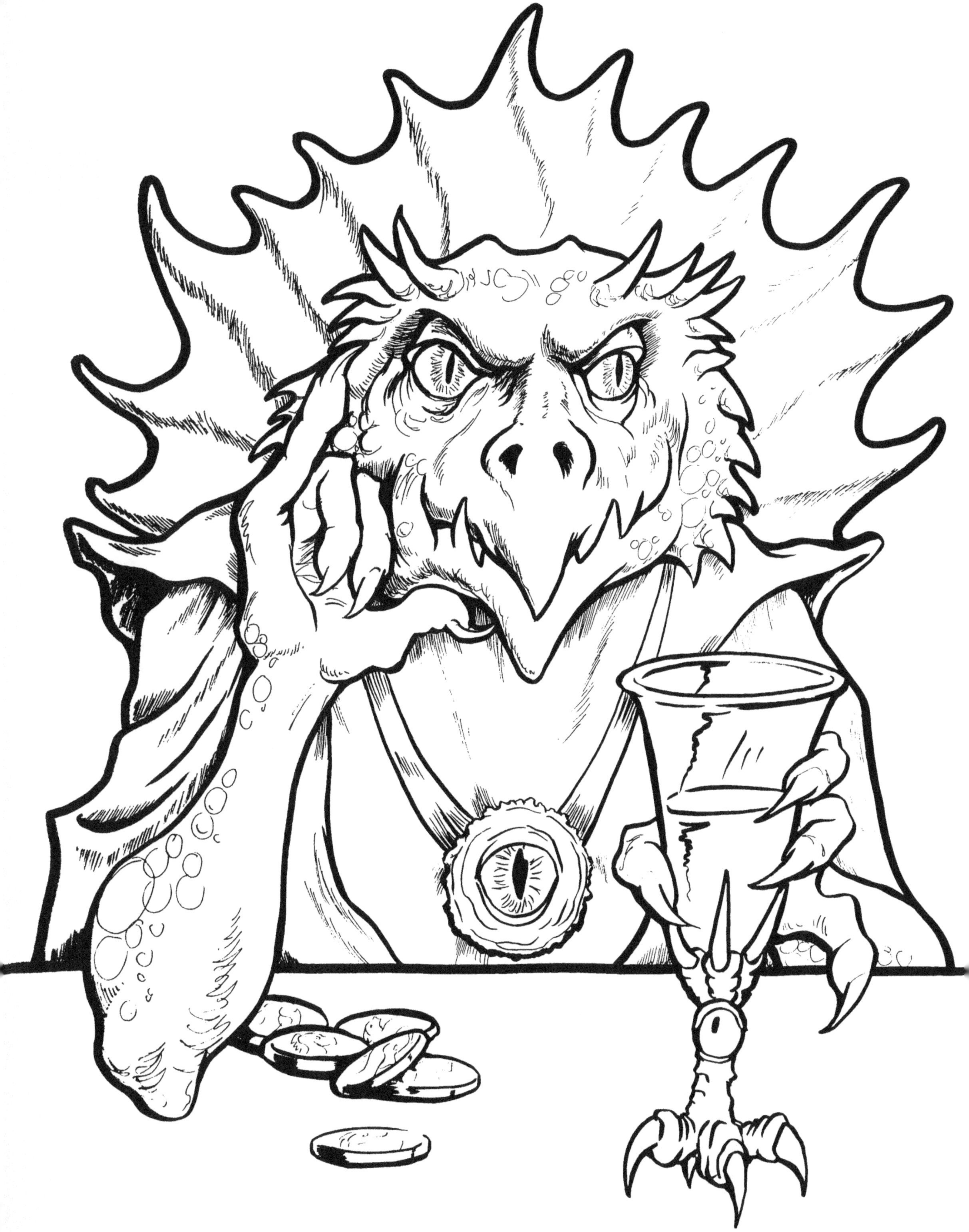

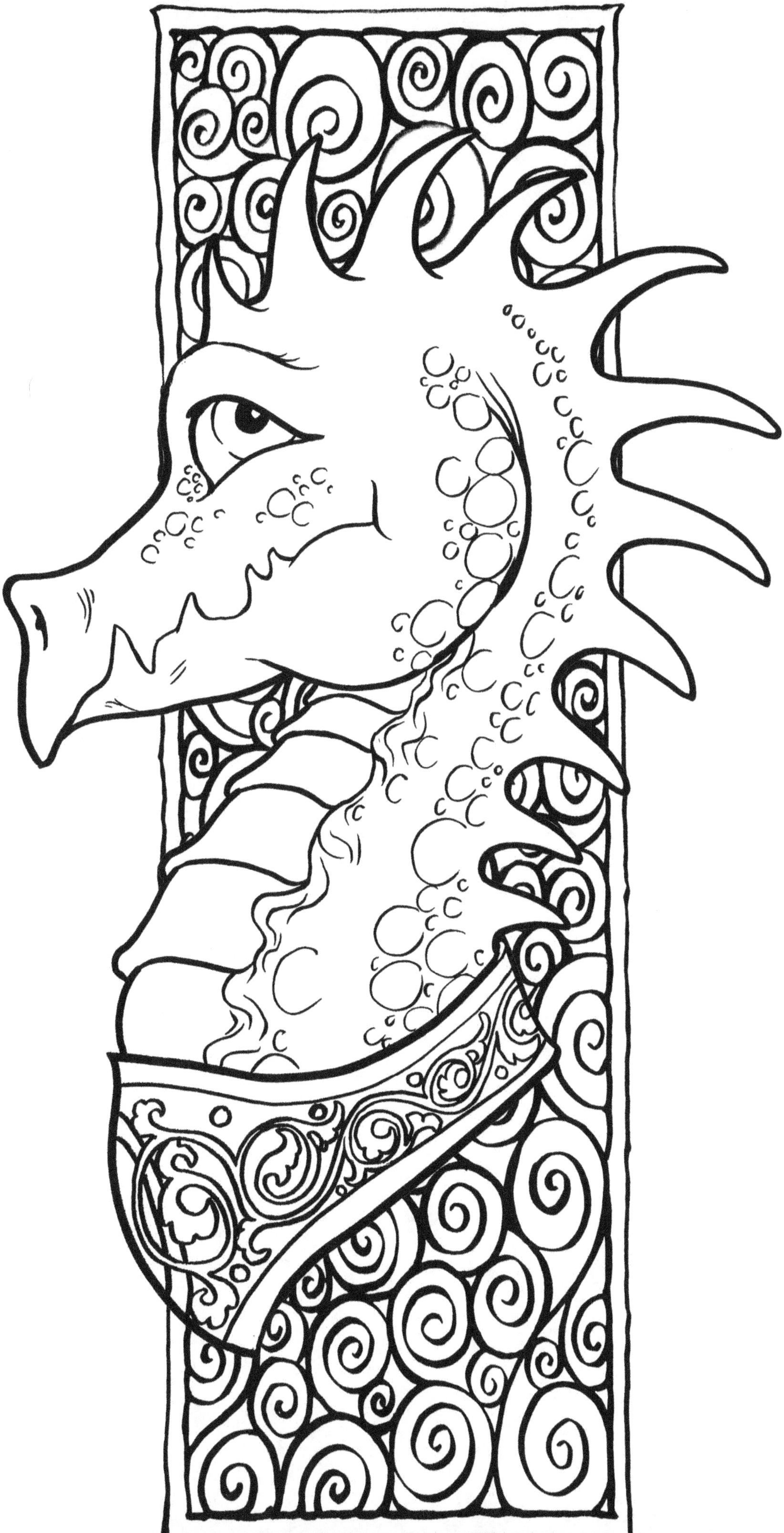

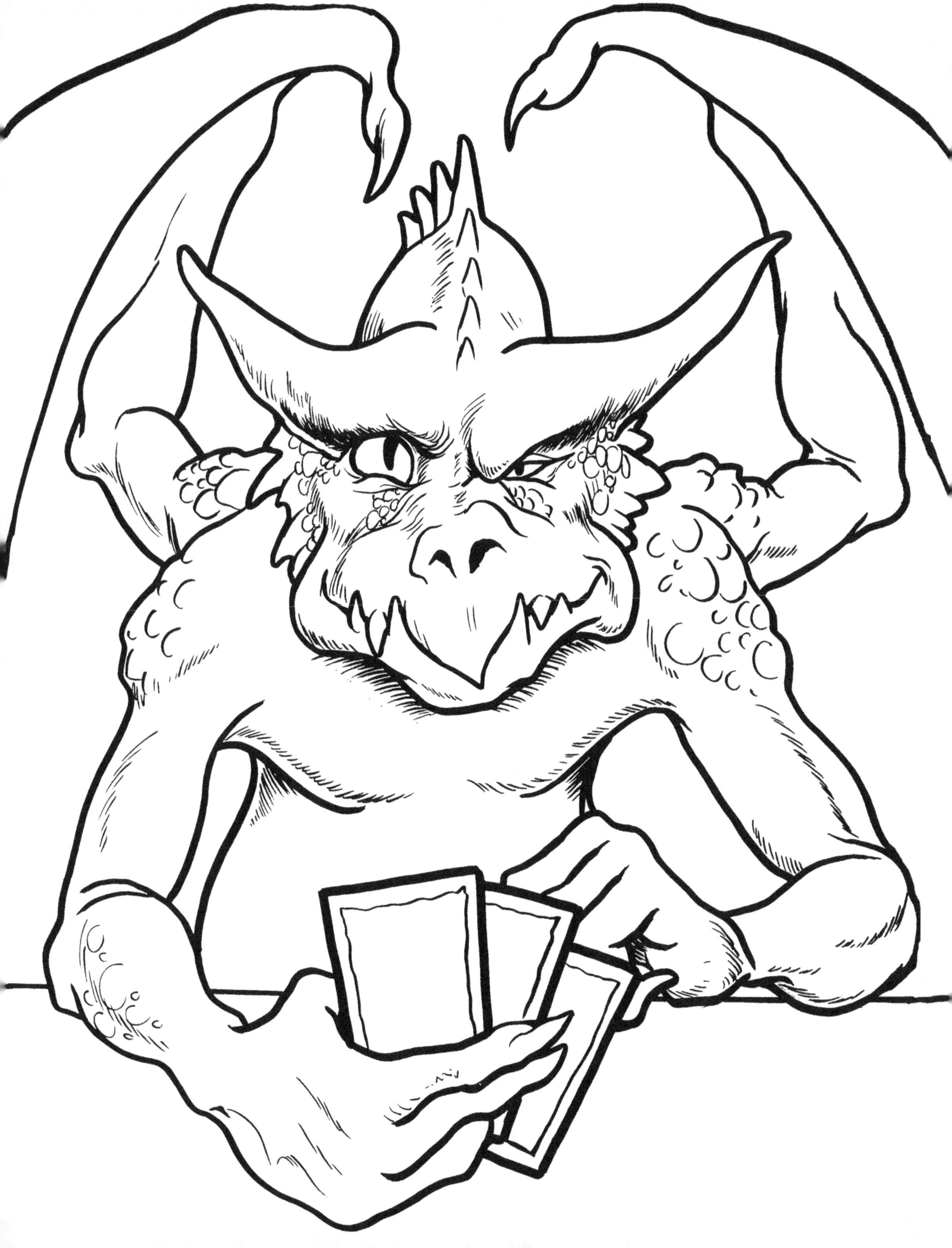

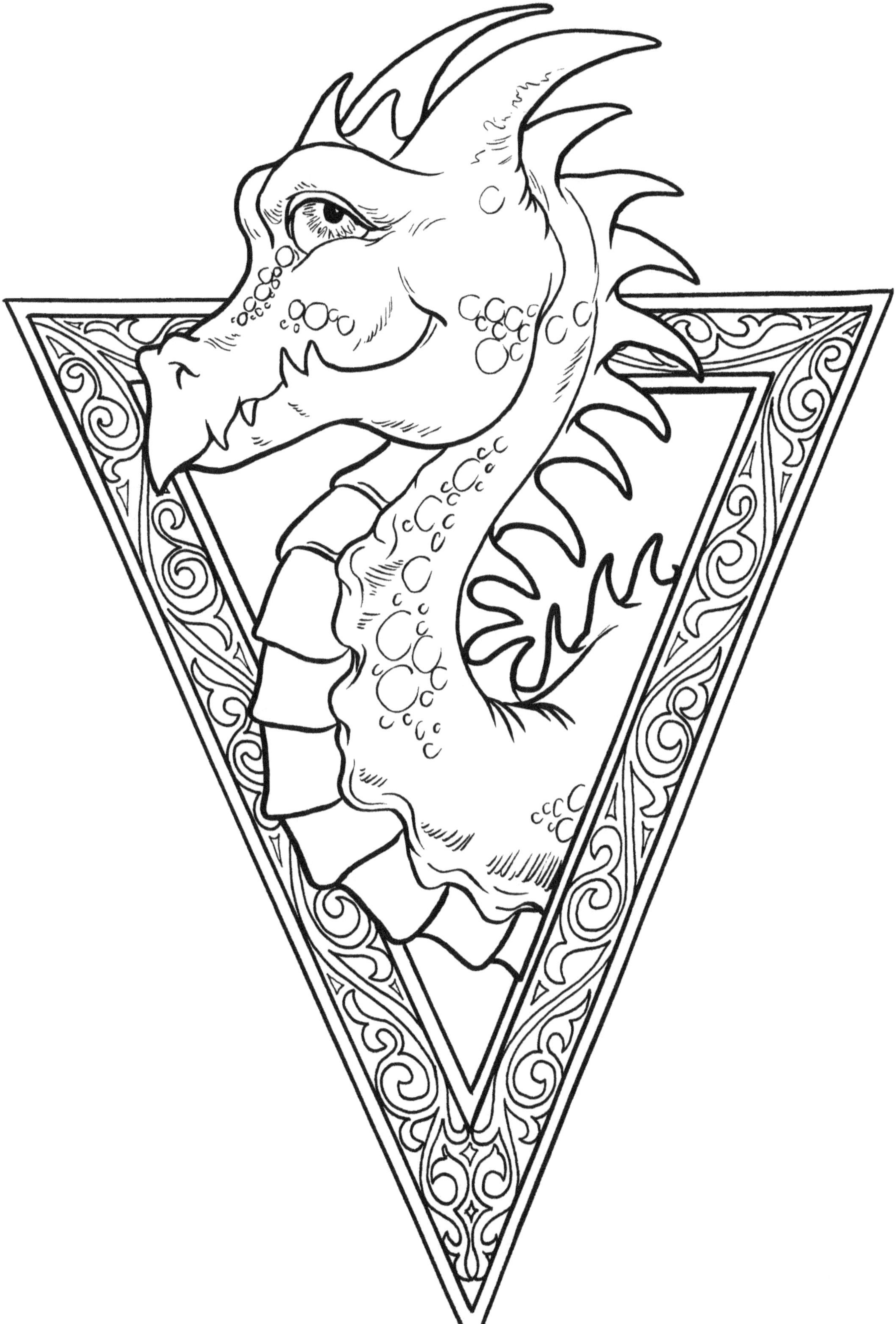

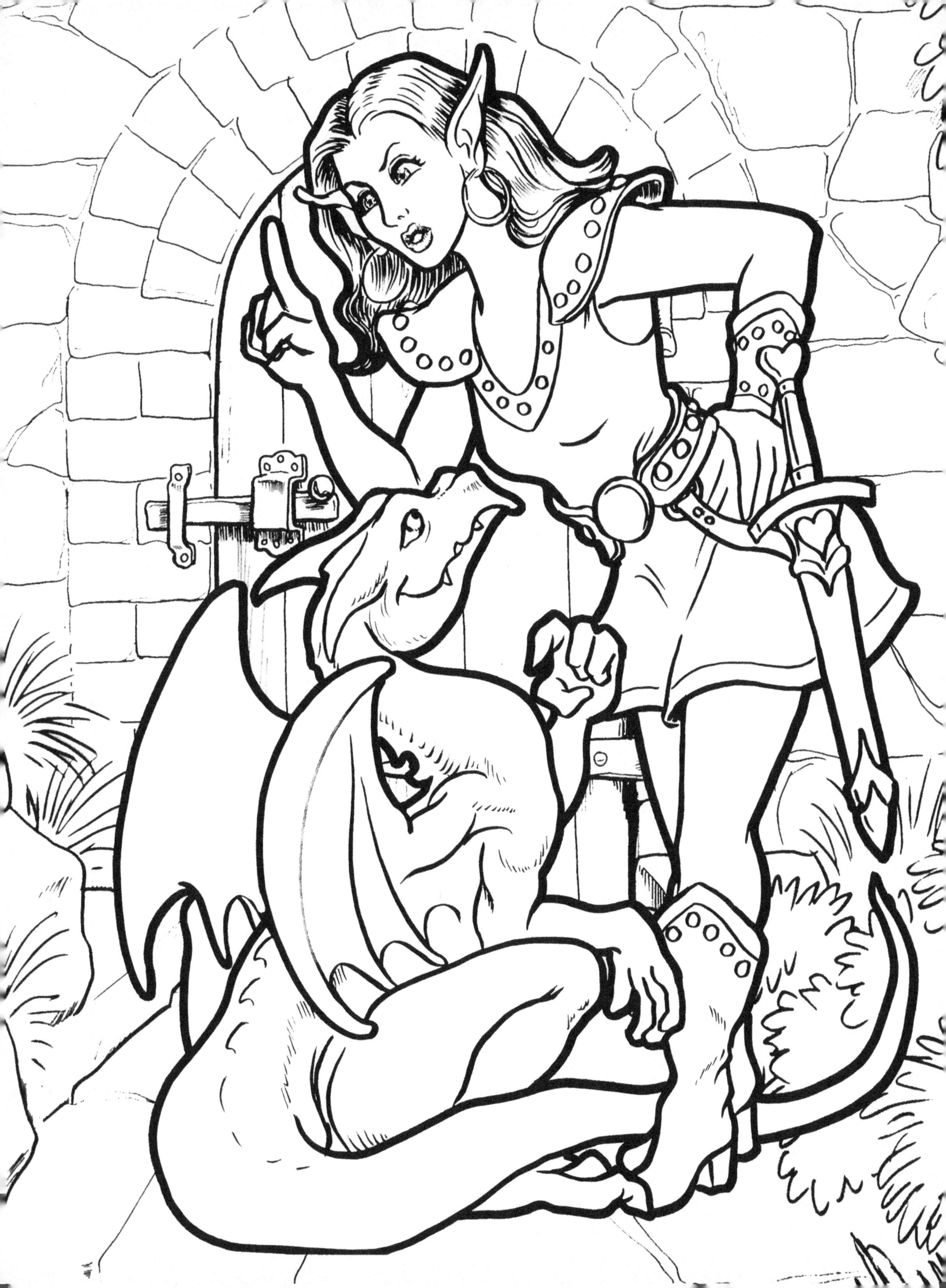

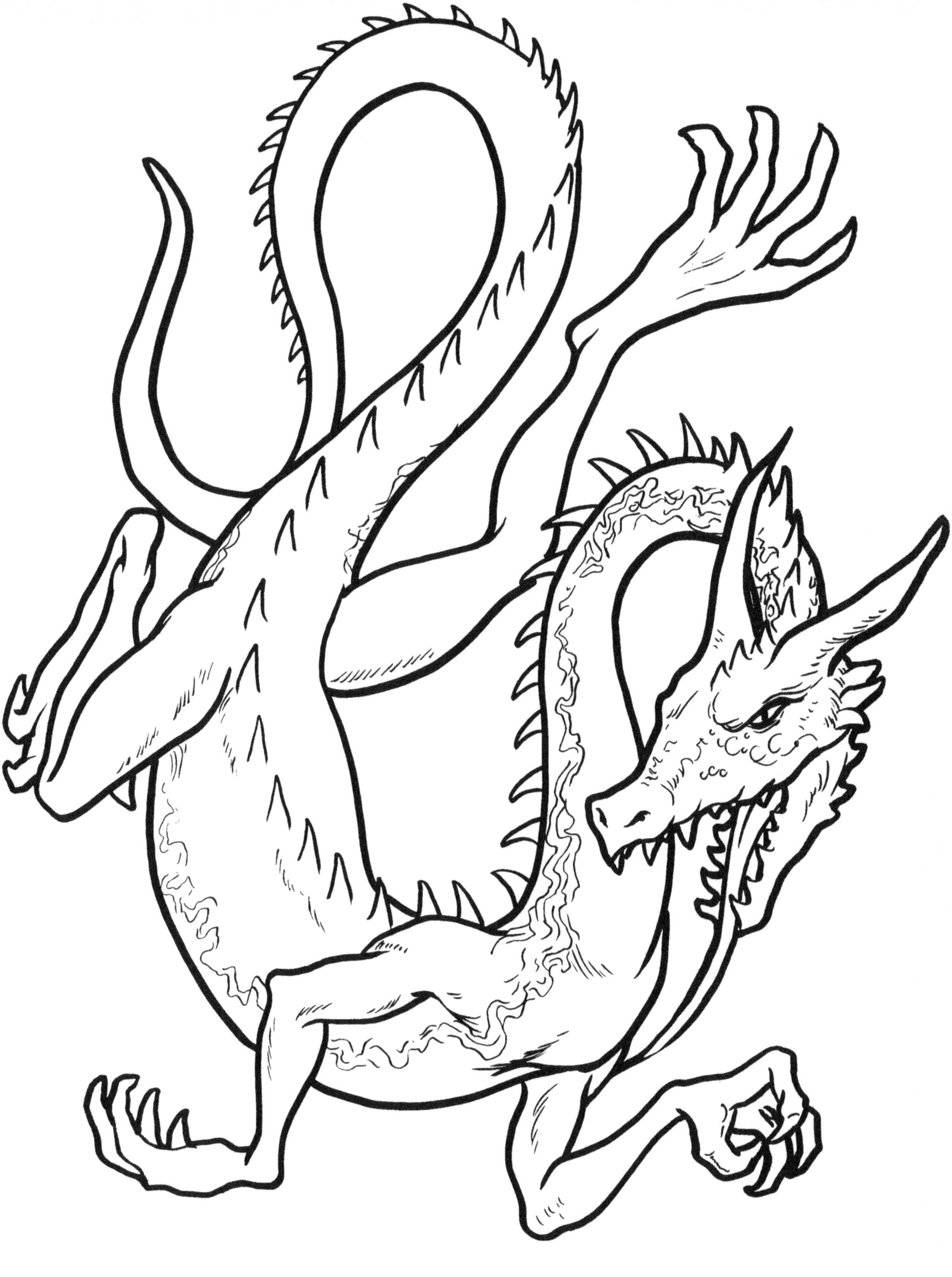

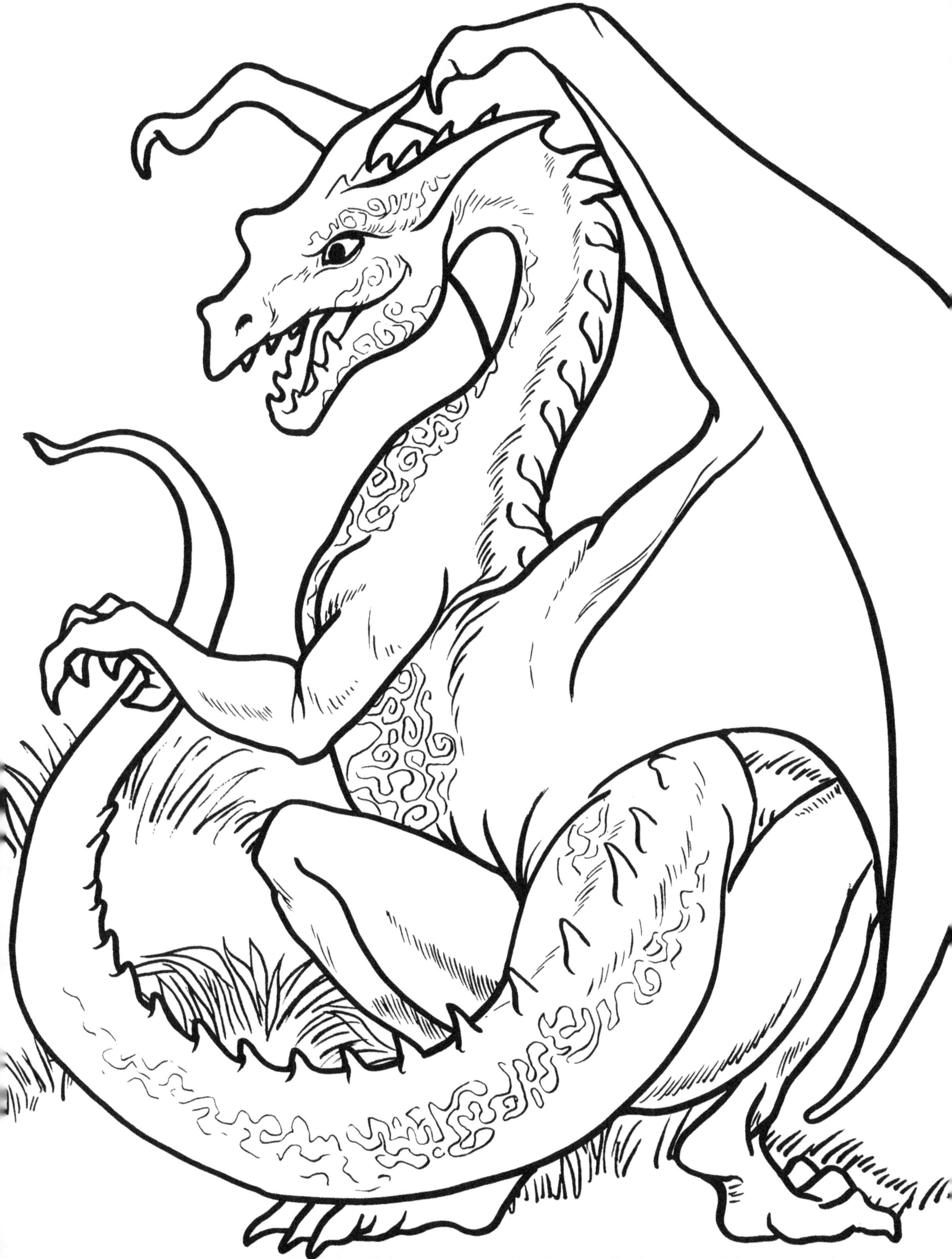

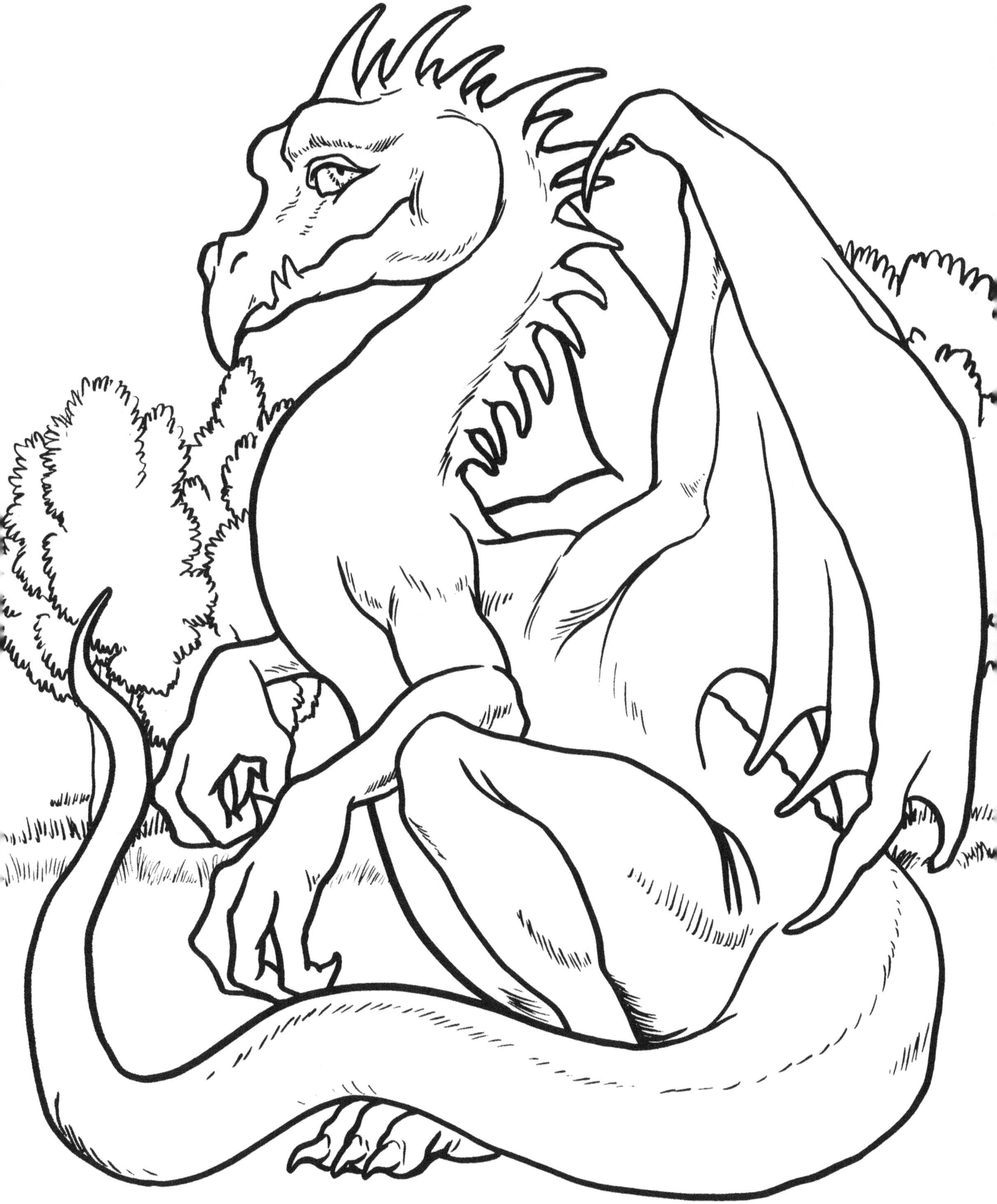

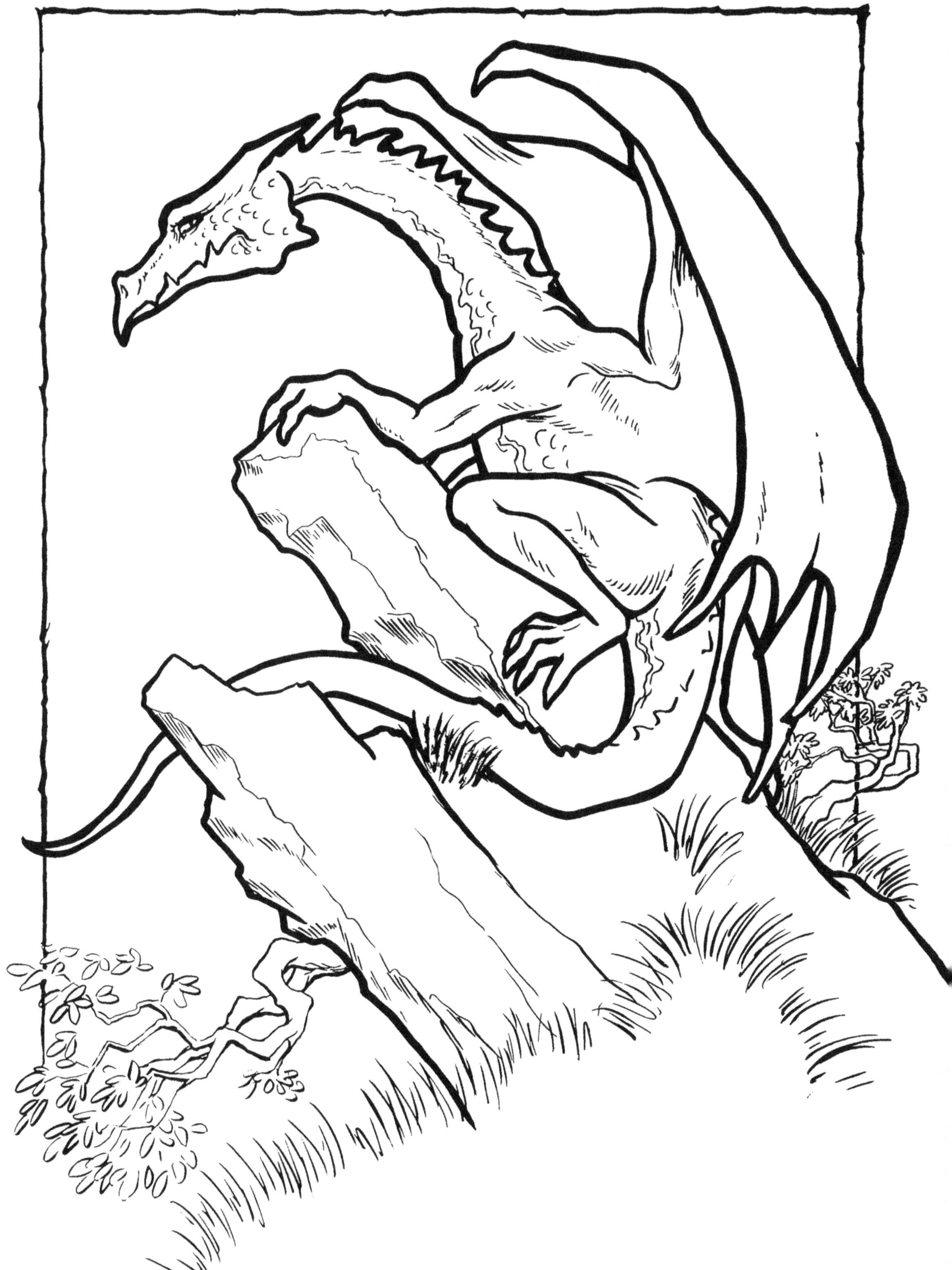

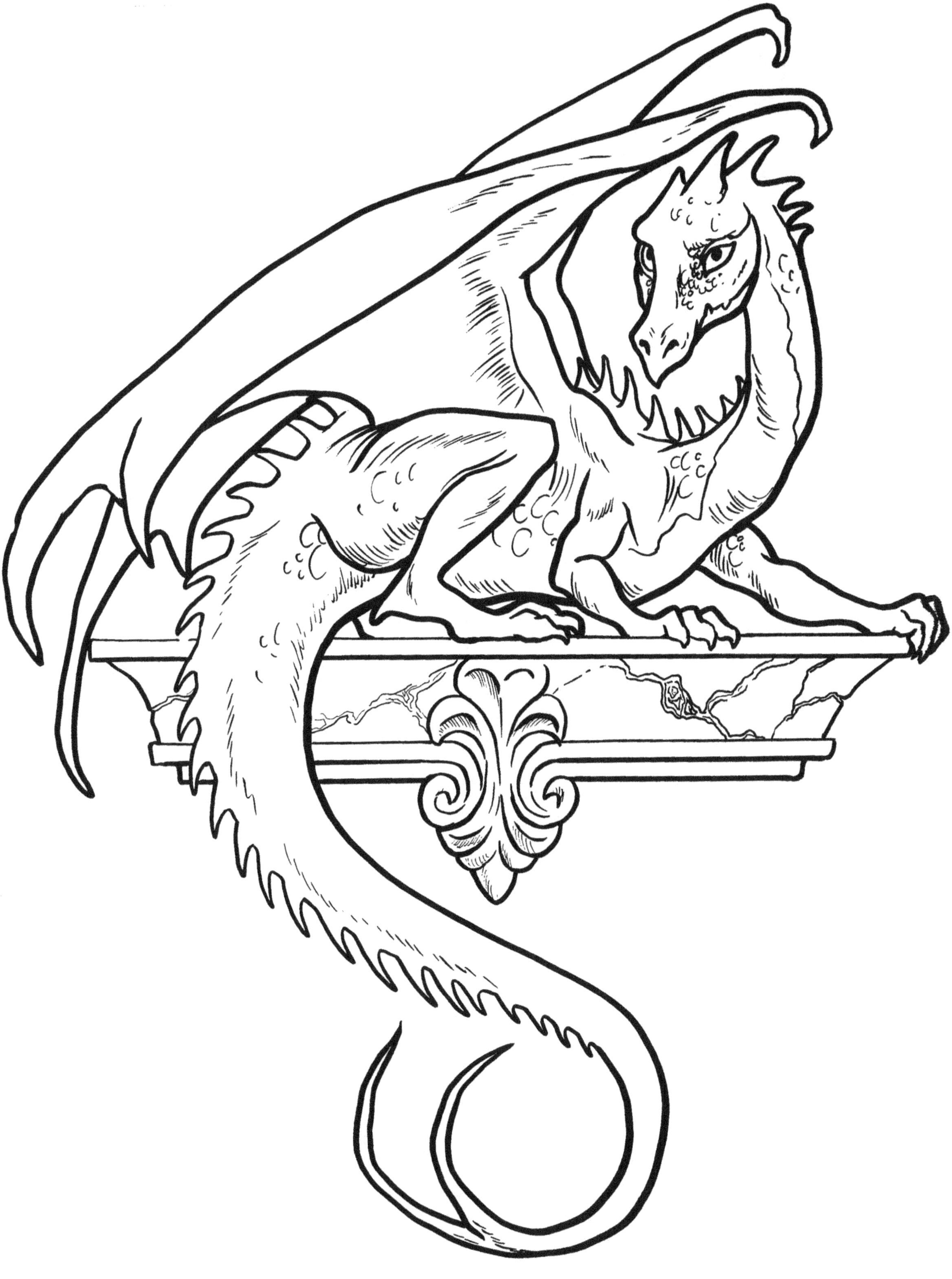

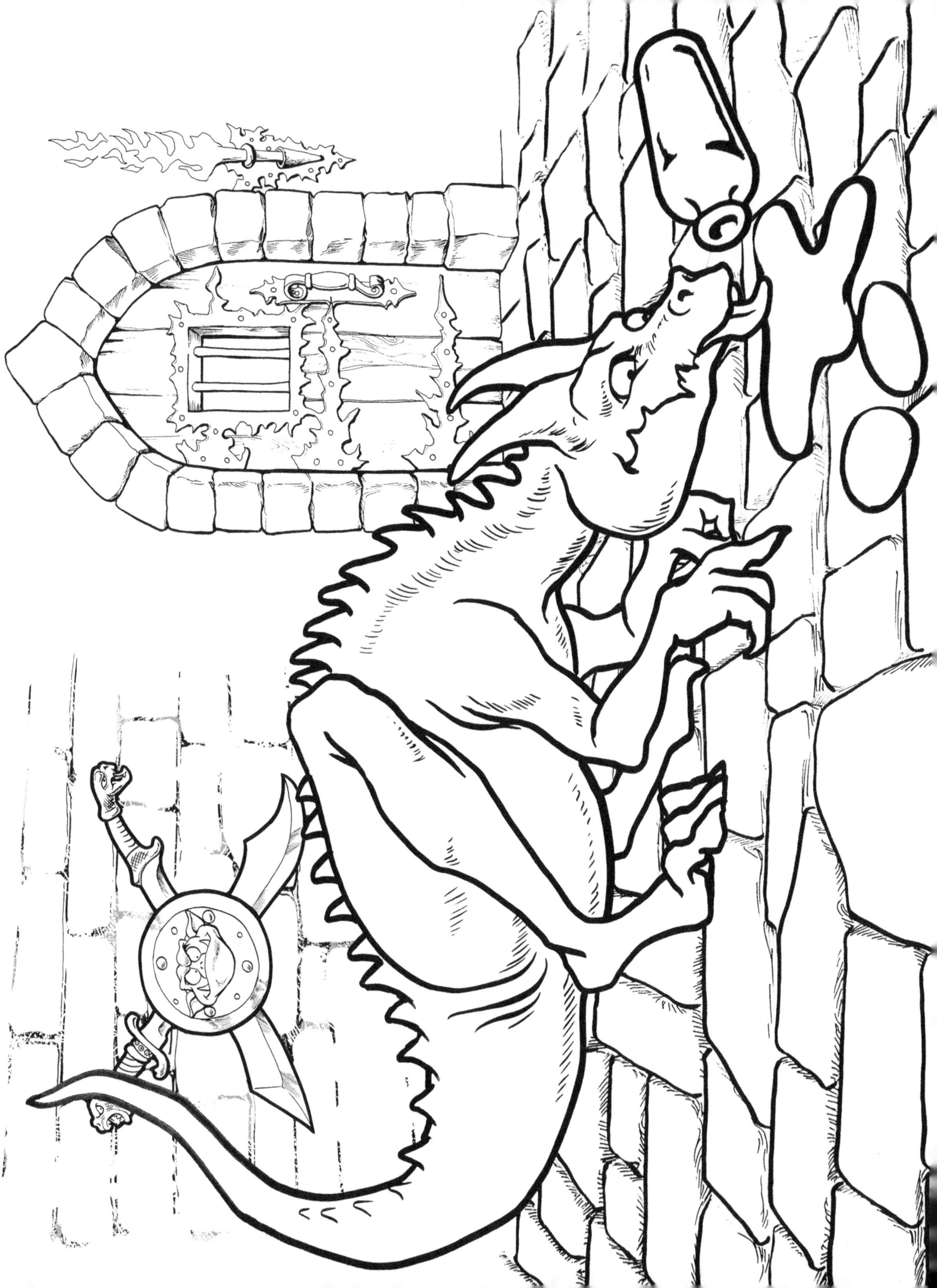

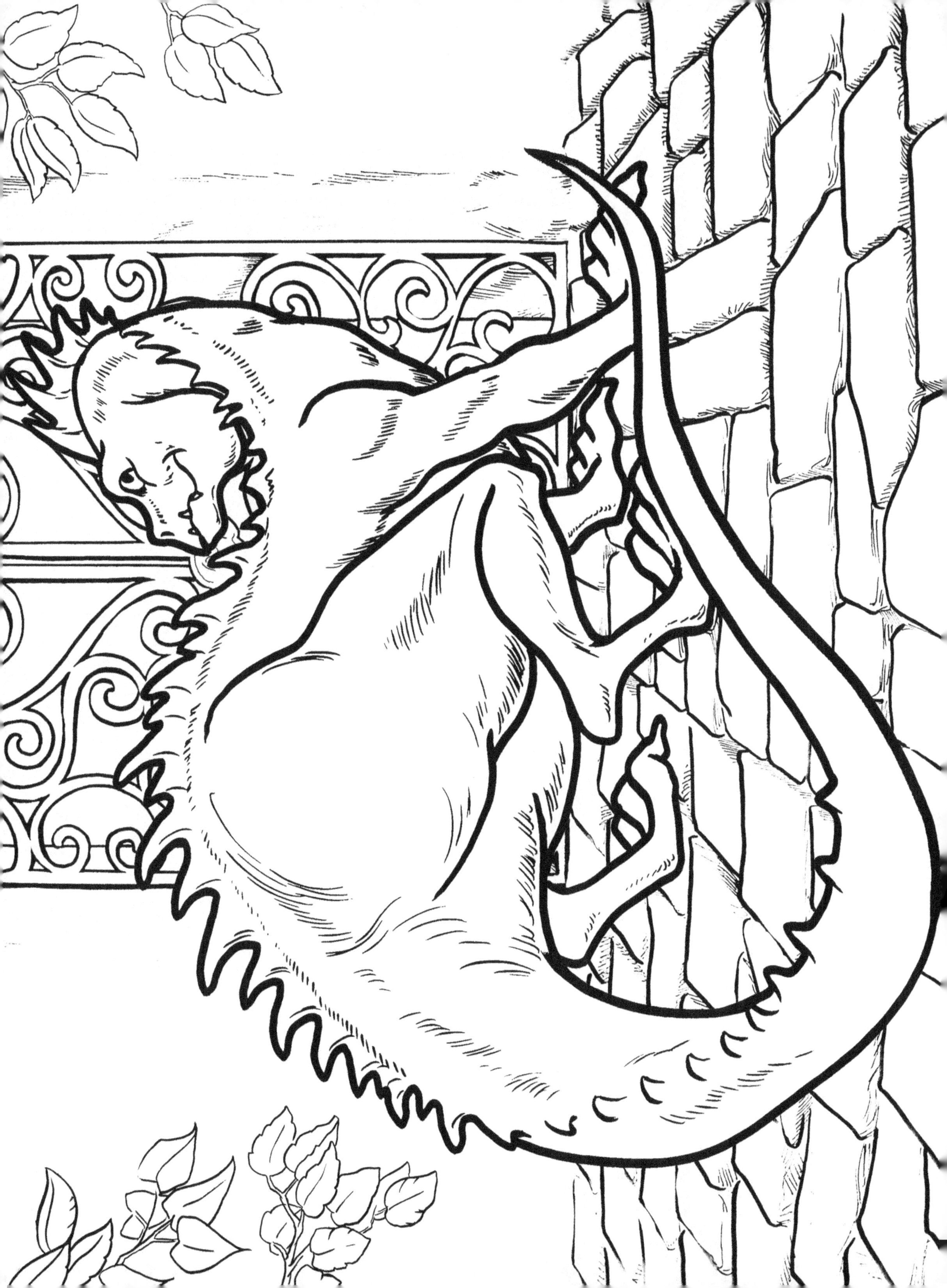

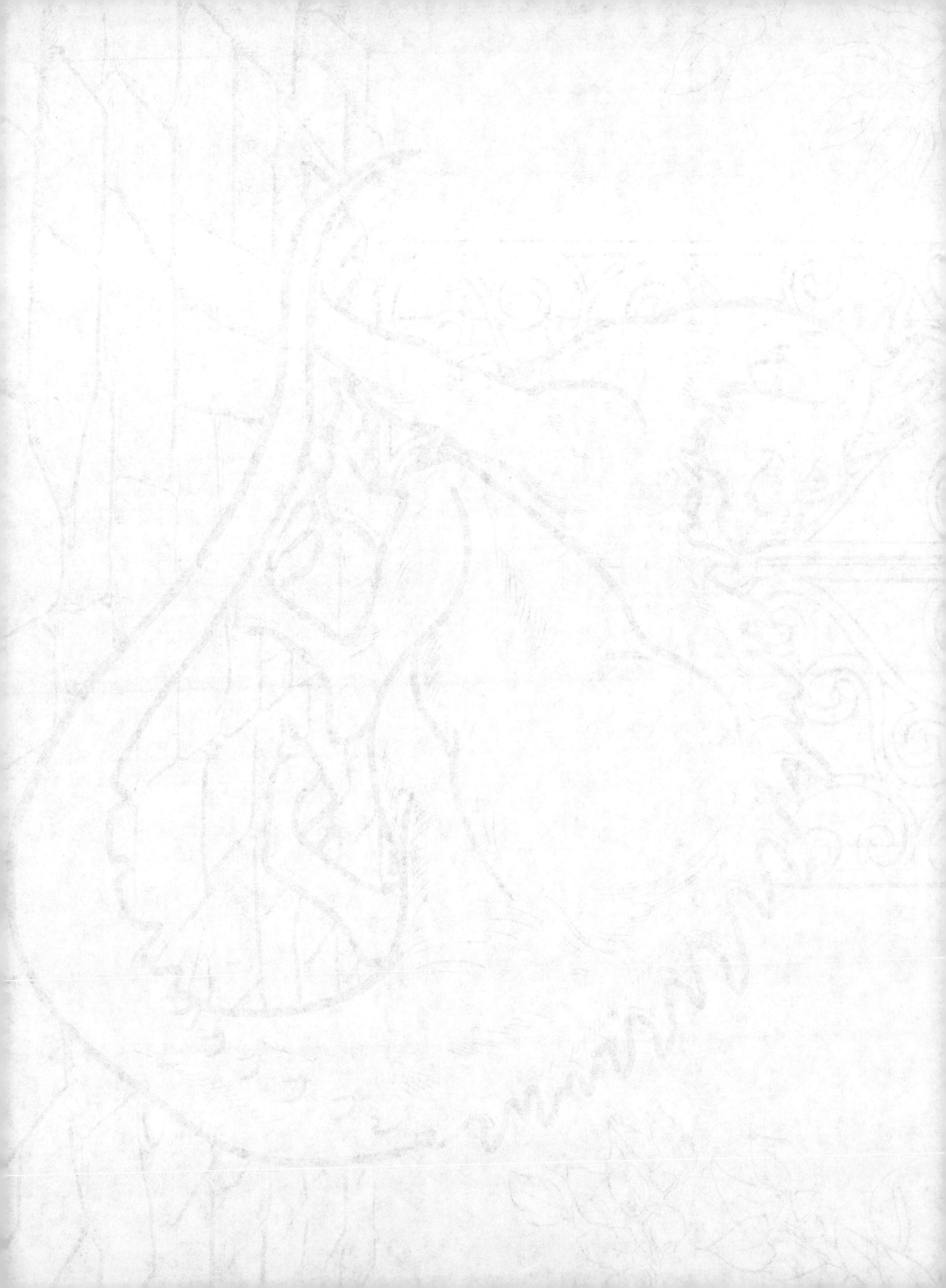

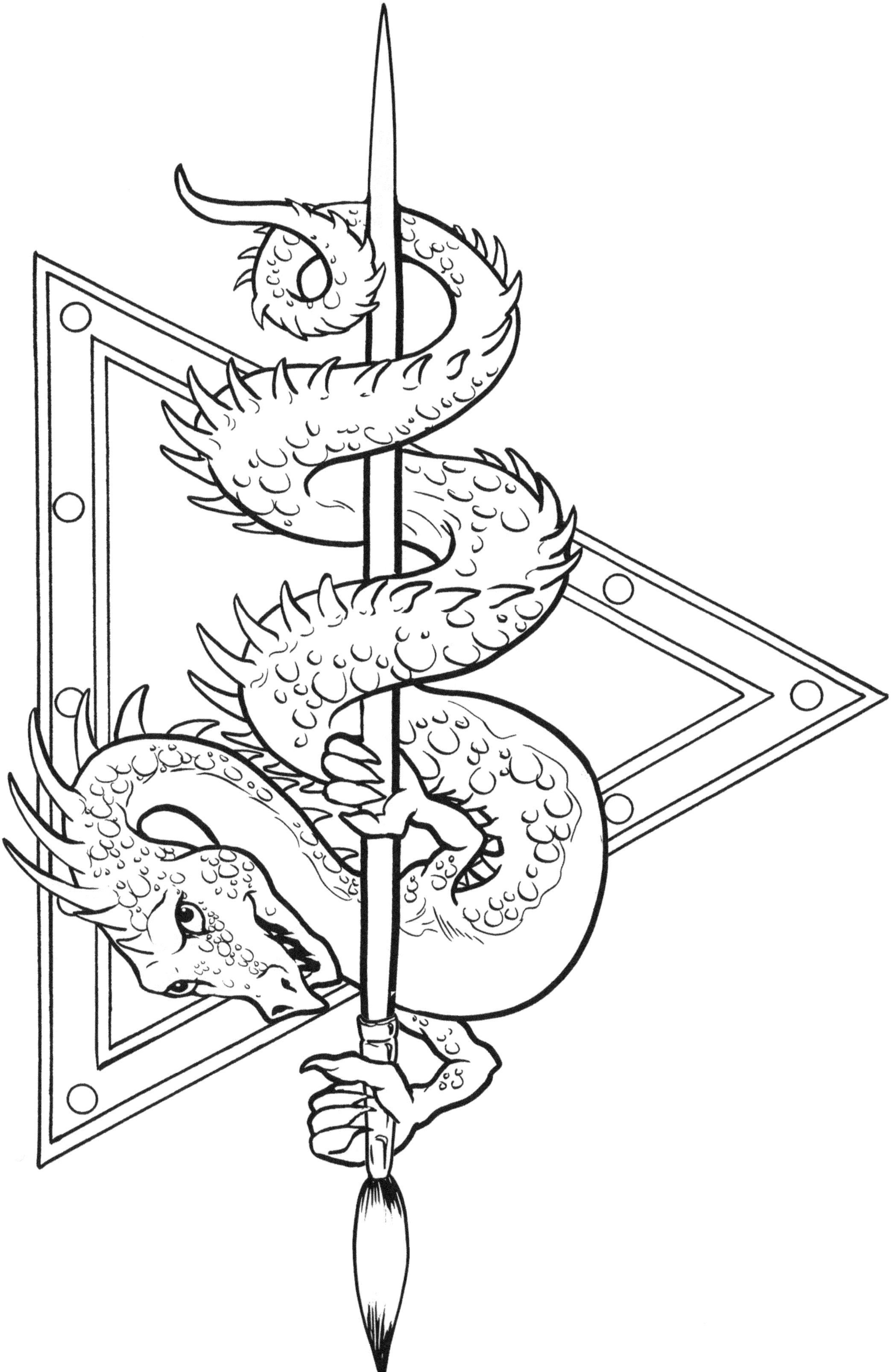

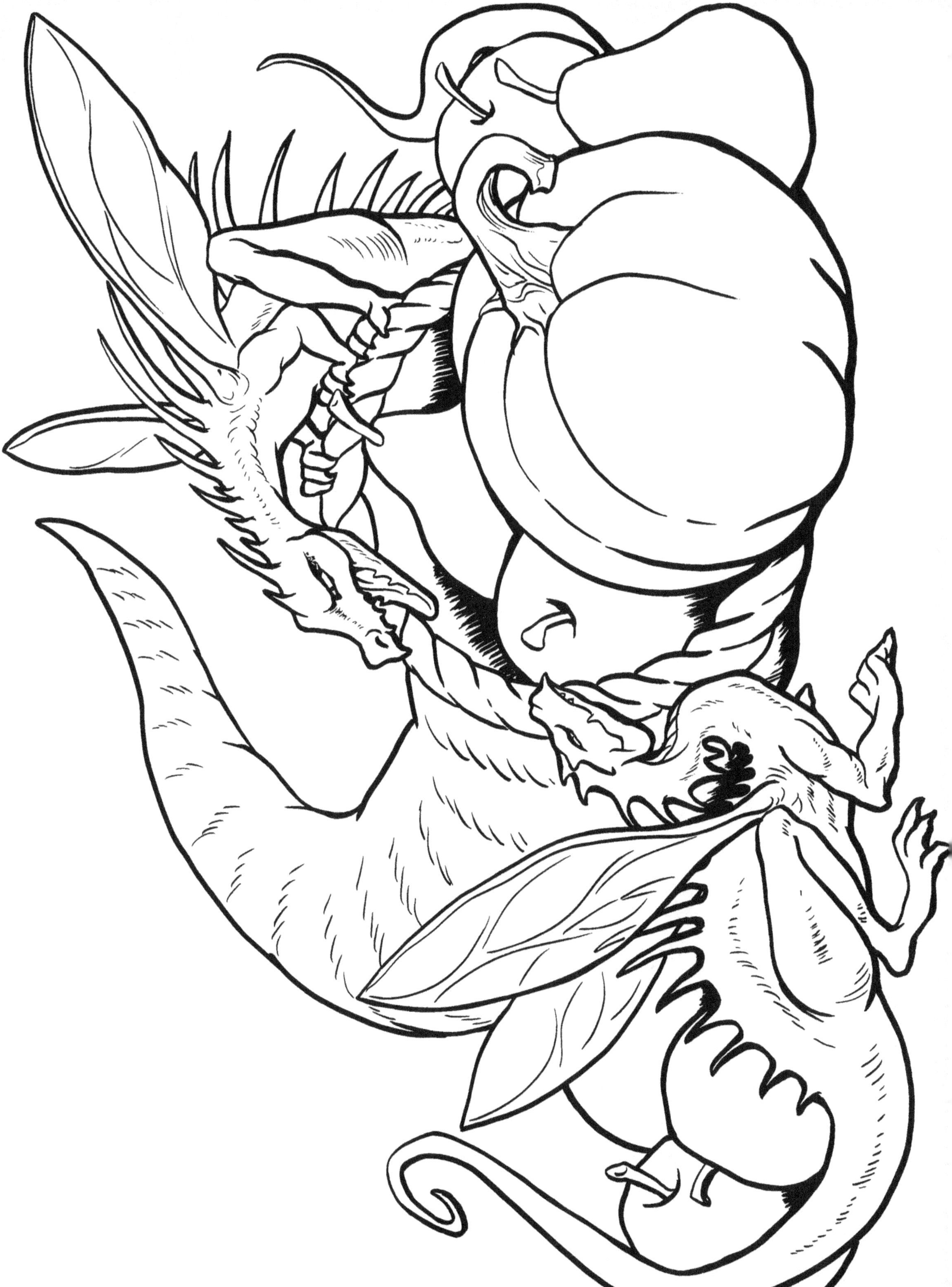

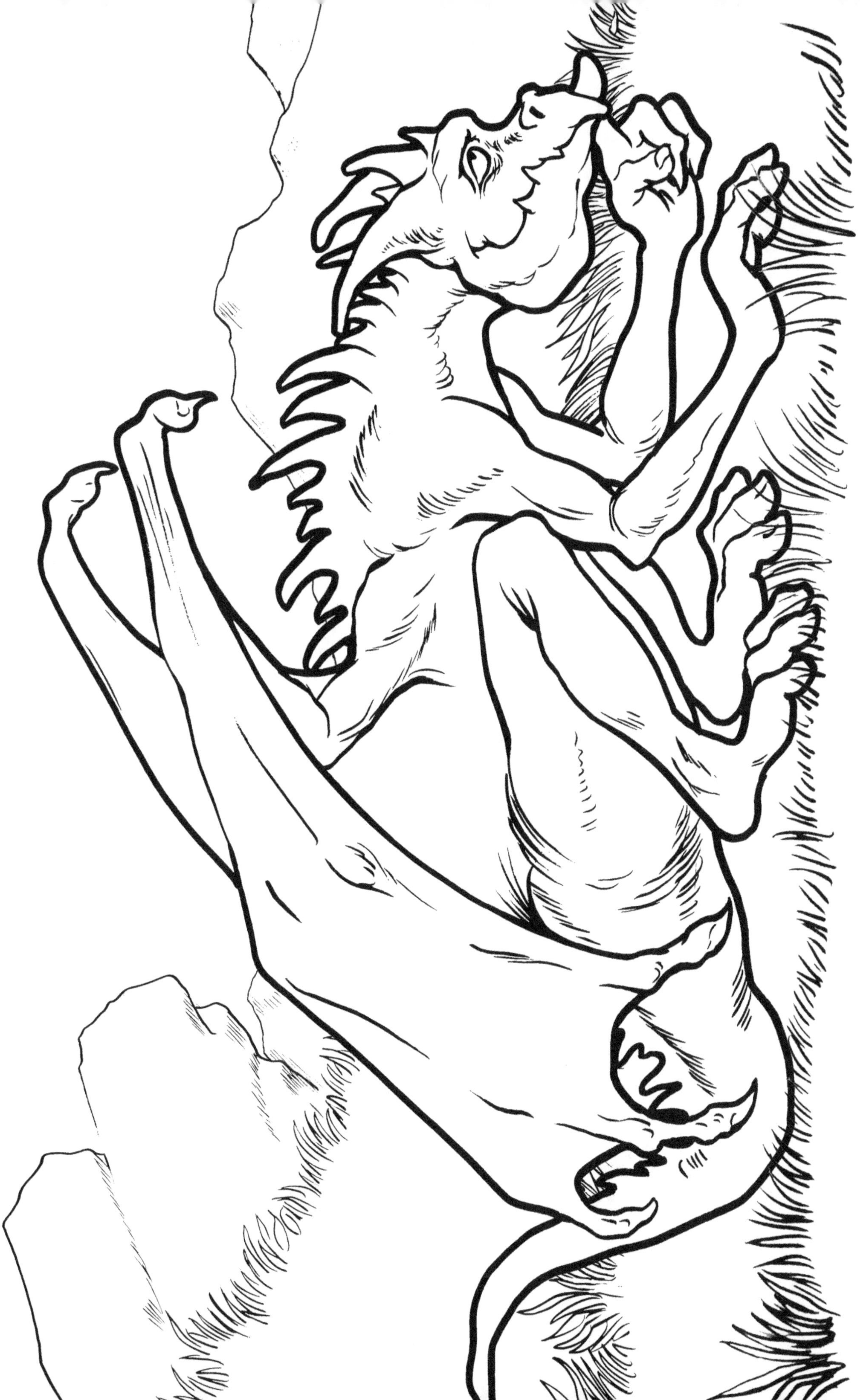

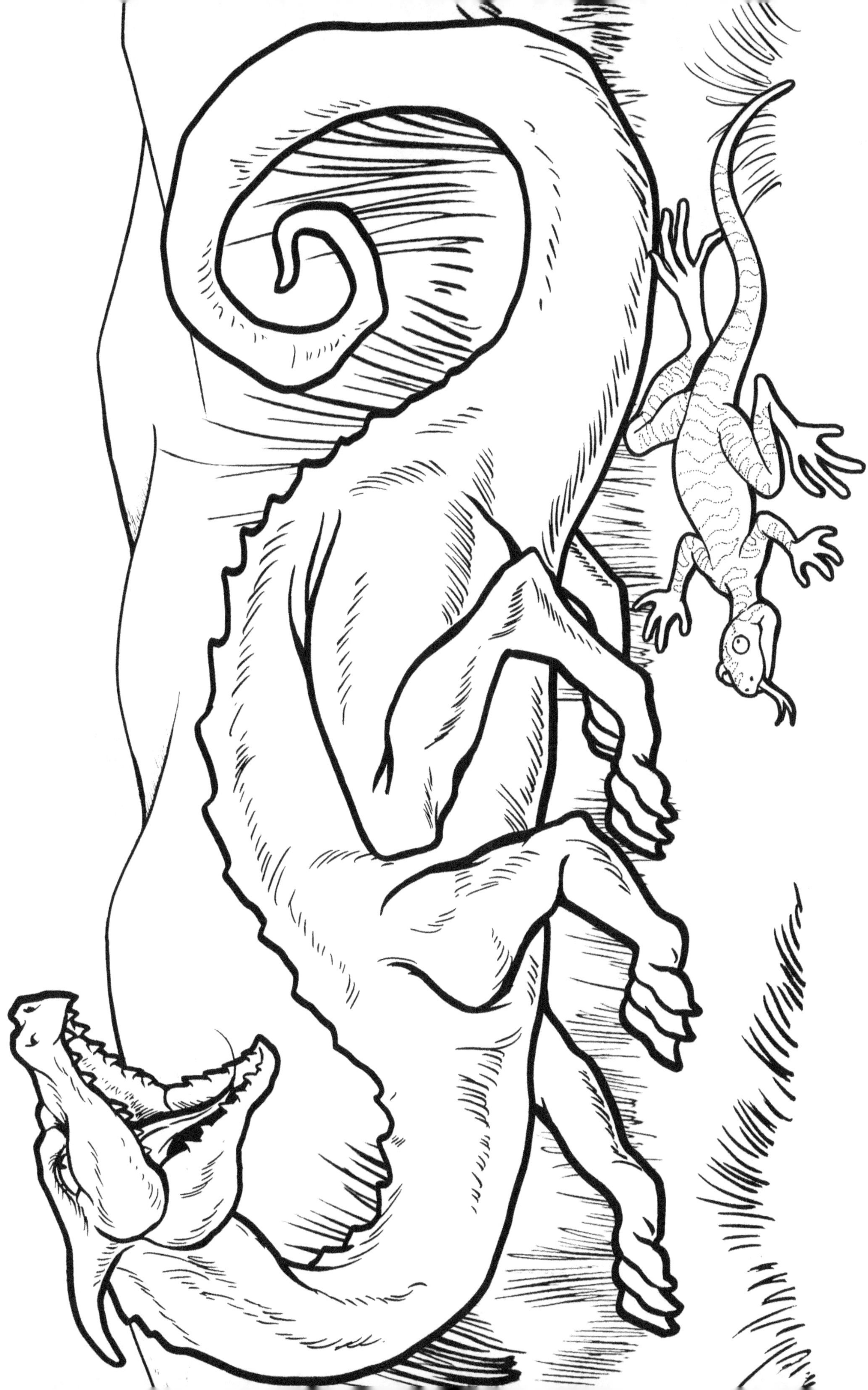

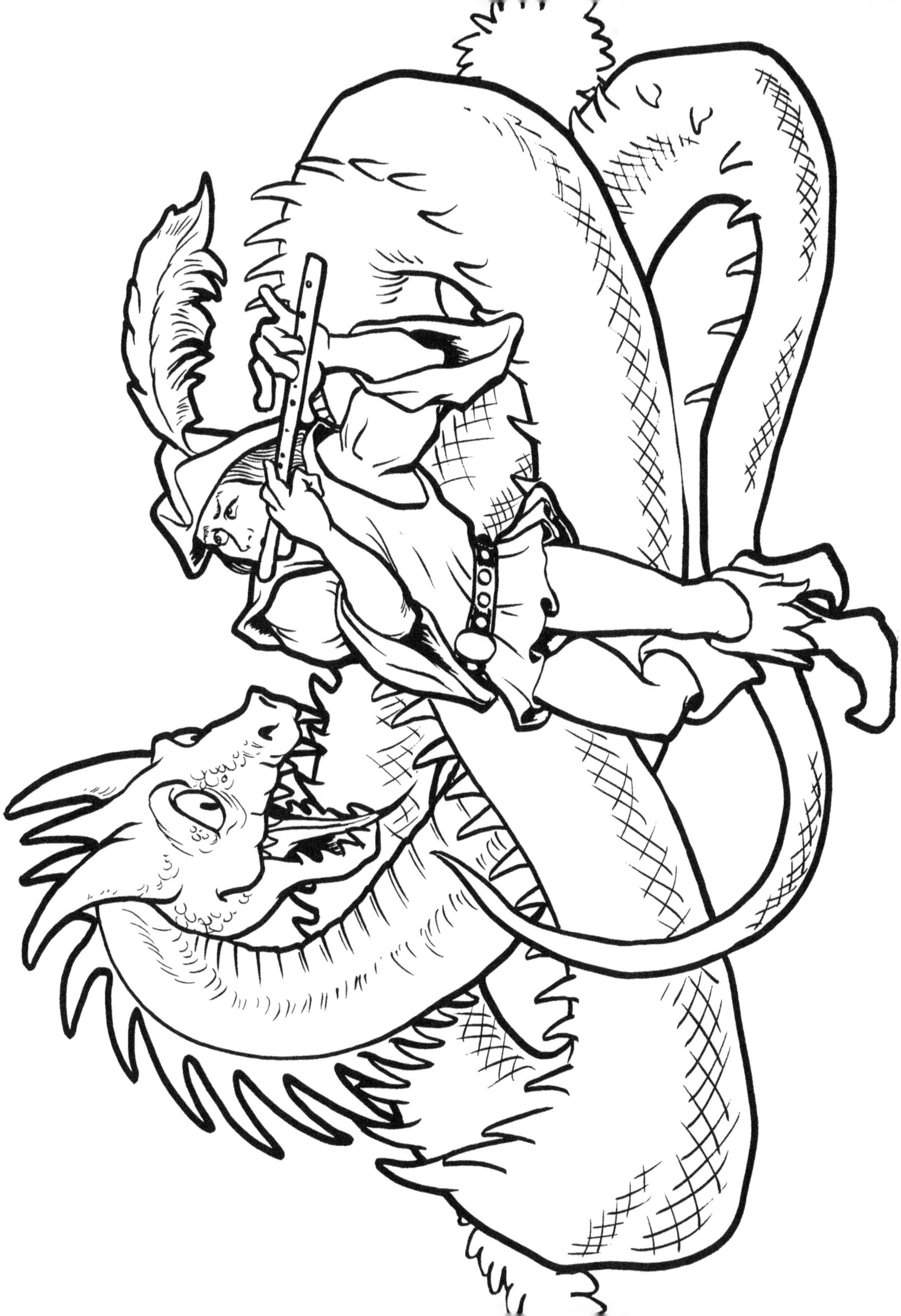

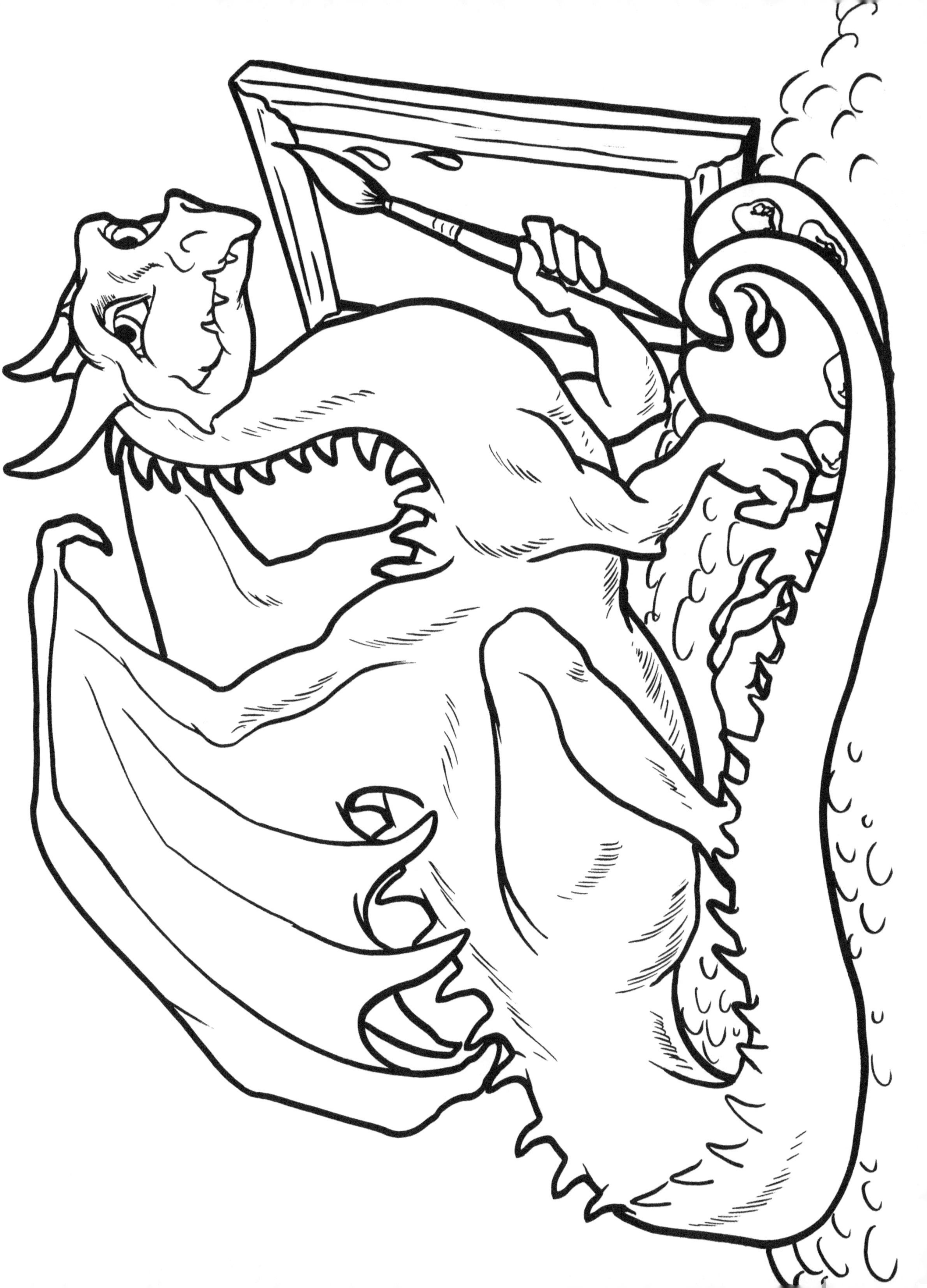

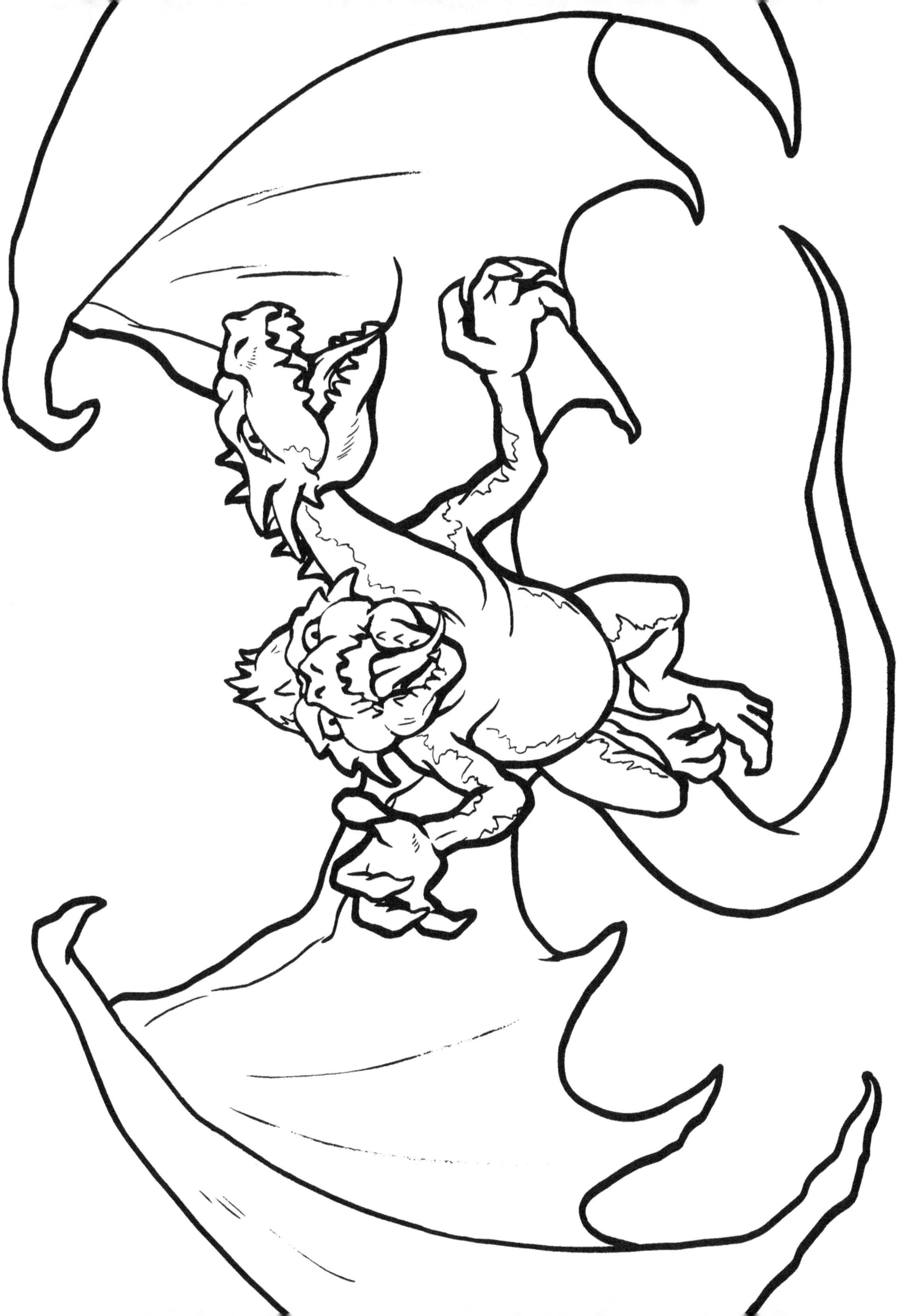

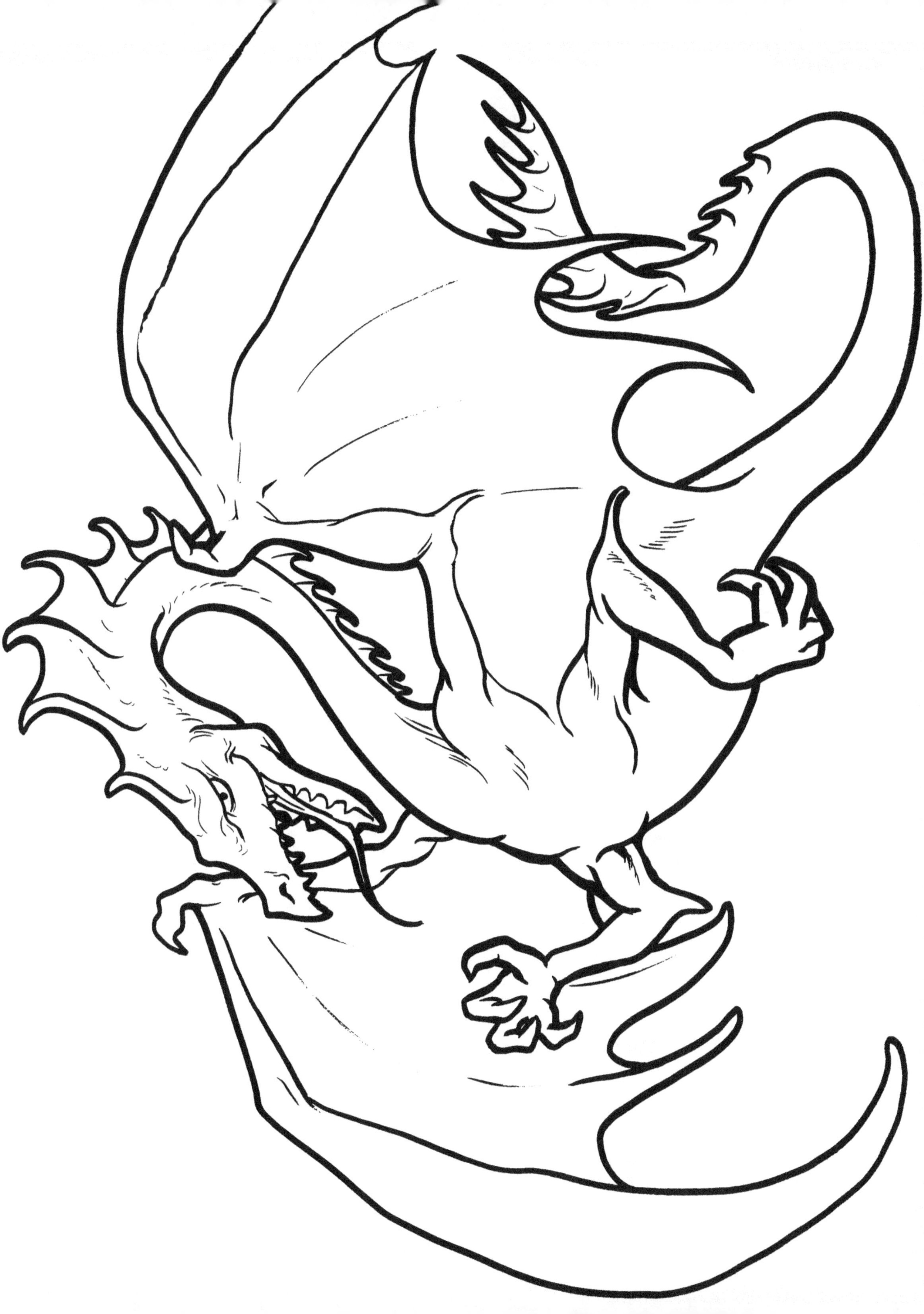

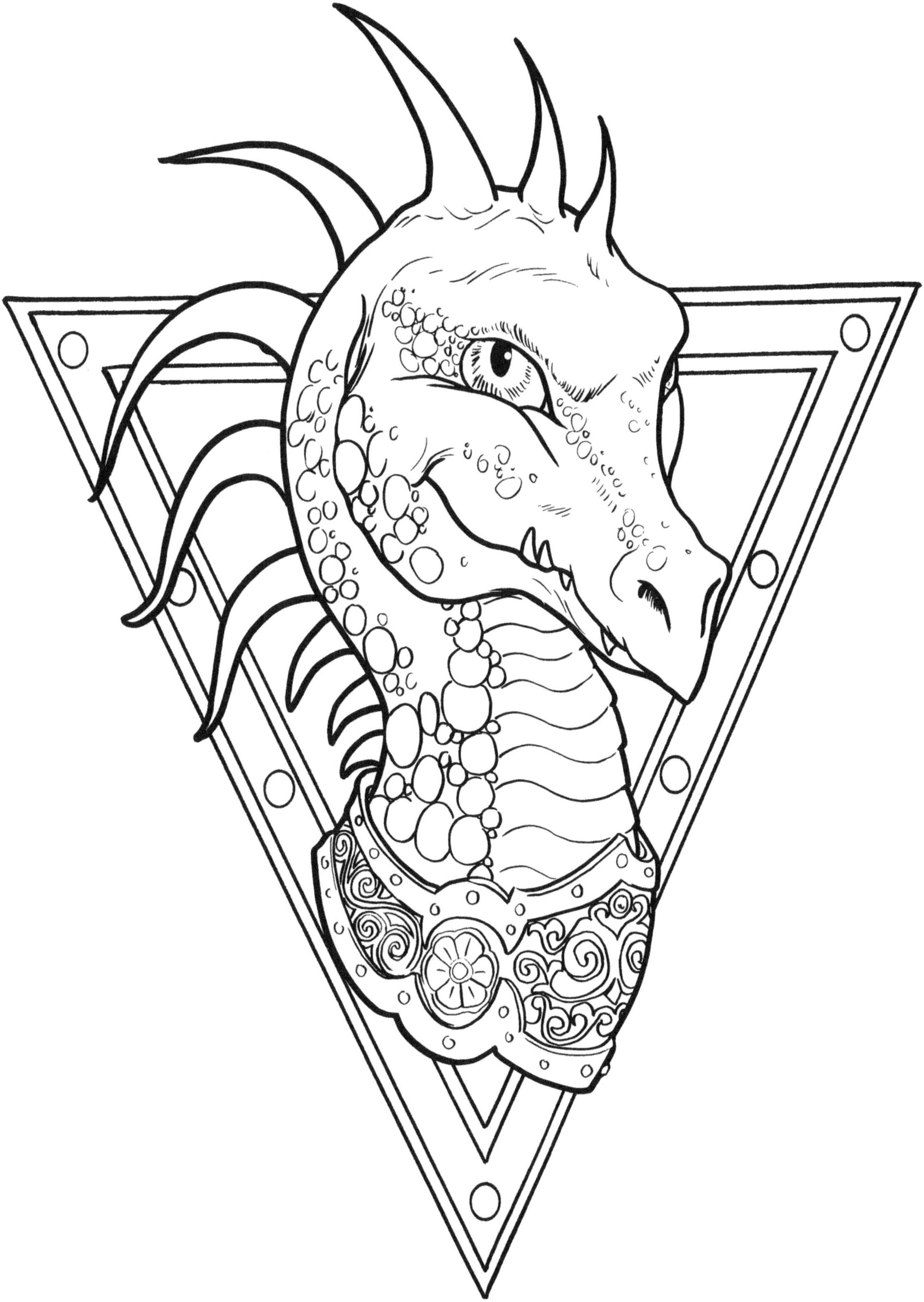

www.ingramcontent.com/pod-product-compliance
Lightning Source LLC
Chambersburg PA
CBHW080611180526
45168CB00007B/2874